Teacher Planner

WEEKLY & MONTHLY LESSON PLAN

NAME: _____

CLASSROOM: _____

EMAIL: _____

PHONE: _____

EMMELINE *eb* BLOOM

Year at a Glance

AUGUST 2021

S	M	T	W	T	F	S
1	2	3	4	5	6	7
8	9	10	11	12	13	14
15	16	17	18	19	20	21
22	23	24	25	26	27	28
29	30	31				

SEPTEMBER 2021

S	M	T	W	T	F	S
			1	2	3	4
5	6	7	8	9	10	11
12	13	14	15	16	17	18
19	20	21	22	23	24	25
26	27	28	29	30		

OCTOBER 2021

S	M	T	W	T	F	S
					1	2
3	4	5	6	7	8	9
10	11	12	13	14	15	16
17	18	19	20	21	22	23
24	25	26	27	28	29	30
31						

NOVEMBER 2021

S	M	T	W	T	F	S
	1	2	3	4	5	6
7	8	9	10	11	12	13
14	15	16	17	18	19	20
21	22	23	24	25	26	27
28	29	30				

DECEMBER 2021

S	M	T	W	T	F	S
			1	2	3	4
5	6	7	8	9	10	11
12	13	14	15	16	17	18
19	20	21	22	23	24	25
26	27	28	29	30	31	

JANUARY 2022

S	M	T	W	T	F	S
						1
2	3	4	5	6	7	8
9	10	11	12	13	14	15
16	17	18	19	20	21	22
23	24	25	26	27	28	29
30	31					

FEBRUARY 2022

S	M	T	W	T	F	S
		1	2	3	4	5
6	7	8	9	10	11	12
13	14	15	16	17	18	19
20	21	22	23	24	25	26
27	28					

MARCH 2022

S	M	T	W	T	F	S
		1	2	3	4	5
6	7	8	9	10	11	12
13	14	15	16	17	18	19
20	21	22	23	24	25	26
27	28	29	30	31		

APRIL 2022

S	M	T	W	T	F	S
					1	2
3	4	5	6	7	8	9
10	11	12	13	14	15	16
17	18	19	20	21	22	23
24	25	26	27	28	29	30

MAY 2022

S	M	T	W	T	F	S
1	2	3	4	5	6	7
8	9	10	11	12	13	14
15	16	17	18	19	20	21
22	23	24	25	26	27	28
29	30	31				

JUNE 2022

S	M	T	W	T	F	S
			1	2	3	4
5	6	7	8	9	10	11
12	13	14	15	16	17	18
19	20	21	22	23	24	25
26	27	28	29	30		

JULY 2022

S	M	T	W	T	F	S
					1	2
3	4	5	6	7	8	9
10	11	12	13	14	15	16
17	18	19	20	21	22	23
24	25	26	27	28	29	30
31						

Notes

_____
_____
_____
_____
_____
_____
_____
_____
_____
_____
_____

Important Dates

AUGUST

_____ _____
_____ _____
_____ _____
_____ _____
_____ _____
_____ _____

SEPTEMBER

_____ _____
_____ _____
_____ _____
_____ _____
_____ _____
_____ _____

OCTOBER

_____ _____
_____ _____
_____ _____
_____ _____
_____ _____
_____ _____

NOVEMBER

_____ _____
_____ _____
_____ _____
_____ _____
_____ _____
_____ _____

DECEMBER

_____ _____
_____ _____
_____ _____
_____ _____
_____ _____
_____ _____

JANUARY

_____ _____
_____ _____
_____ _____
_____ _____
_____ _____
_____ _____

FEBRUARY

_____ _____
_____ _____
_____ _____
_____ _____
_____ _____

MARCH

_____ _____
_____ _____
_____ _____
_____ _____
_____ _____

APRIL

_____ _____
_____ _____
_____ _____
_____ _____
_____ _____

MAY

_____ _____
_____ _____
_____ _____
_____ _____
_____ _____

JUNE

_____ _____
_____ _____
_____ _____
_____ _____
_____ _____

JULY

_____ _____
_____ _____
_____ _____
_____ _____
_____ _____

Birthdays

AUGUST

_____ _____
_____ _____
_____ _____
_____ _____
_____ _____
_____ _____
_____ _____

SEPTEMBER

_____ _____
_____ _____
_____ _____
_____ _____
_____ _____
_____ _____
_____ _____

OCTOBER

_____ _____
_____ _____
_____ _____
_____ _____
_____ _____
_____ _____
_____ _____

NOVEMBER

_____ _____
_____ _____
_____ _____
_____ _____
_____ _____
_____ _____
_____ _____

DECEMBER

_____ _____
_____ _____
_____ _____
_____ _____
_____ _____
_____ _____
_____ _____

JANUARY

_____ _____
_____ _____
_____ _____
_____ _____
_____ _____
_____ _____
_____ _____

FEBRUARY

_____ _____
_____ _____
_____ _____
_____ _____
_____ _____
_____ _____
_____ _____

MARCH

_____ _____
_____ _____
_____ _____
_____ _____
_____ _____
_____ _____
_____ _____

APRIL

_____ _____
_____ _____
_____ _____
_____ _____
_____ _____
_____ _____
_____ _____

MAY

_____ _____
_____ _____
_____ _____
_____ _____
_____ _____
_____ _____

JUNE

_____ _____
_____ _____
_____ _____
_____ _____
_____ _____
_____ _____

JULY

_____ _____
_____ _____
_____ _____
_____ _____
_____ _____
_____ _____

Class List

FIRST NAME	LAST NAME	NOTES/COMMENTS

Attendance Record

Grade Record

Notes

THE MEANING OF LIFE IS TO FIND YOUR GIFT.
THE PURPOSE OF LIFE IS TO GIVE IT AWAY.

SUNDAY	MONDAY	TUESDAY
01	02	03
08	09	10
15	16	17
22	23	24
29	30	31

AUGUST BANK HOLIDAY (UK)

August 2021

WEDNESDAY	THURSDAY	FRIDAY	SATURDAY
04	05	06	07
11	12	13	14
18	19	20	21
25	26	27	28

July 26 - August 1, 2021

SUBJECT	MONDAY	26	TUESDAY	27	WEDNESDAY	28

Words of Wisdom: I MAKE A DIFFERENCE IN THE WORLD, ONE CHILD AT A TIME.

THURSDAY	29	FRIDAY	30	SATURDAY	31

SUNDAY | 01

GOALS

- ○
- ○
- ○
- ○
- ○
- ○
- ○
- ○

NOTES

August 2 - August 8, 2021

SUBJECT	MONDAY	02	TUESDAY	03	WEDNESDAY	04

THURSDAY	05	FRIDAY	06	SATURDAY	07

SUNDAY 08

GOALS

- ○
- ○
- ○
- ○
- ○
- ○
- ○
- ○

NOTES

August 9 – August 15, 2021

SUBJECT	MONDAY	09	TUESDAY	10	WEDNESDAY	11

Words of Wisdom: IF IT DOESN'T CHALLENGE YOU, IT DOESN'T CHANGE YOU.

THURSDAY	12	FRIDAY	13	SATURDAY	14

SUNDAY   15

GOALS

- ◯
- ◯
- ◯
- ◯
- ◯
- ◯
- ◯
- ◯

NOTES

August 16 - August 22, 2021

SUBJECT	MONDAY	16	TUESDAY	17	WEDNESDAY	18

THURSDAY	19	FRIDAY	20	SATURDAY	21

SUNDAY | 22

GOALS

- ◯
- ◯
- ◯
- ◯
- ◯
- ◯
- ◯
- ◯

NOTES

August 23 - August 29, 2021

SUBJECT	MONDAY	23	TUESDAY	24	WEDNESDAY	25

Words of Wisdom: I TRUST MYSELF TO MAKE THE BEST DECISIONS FOR MY STUDENTS.

THURSDAY	26	FRIDAY	27	SATURDAY	28

SUNDAY 29

GOALS

- ◯
- ◯
- ◯
- ◯
- ◯
- ◯
- ◯
- ◯

NOTES

Notes

_____

_____

_____

_____

_____

_____

_____

_____

_____

_____

_____

_____

_____

_____

_____

_____

_____

_____

_____

_____

_____

_____

_____

THOSE WHO BELIEVE IN THEIR DREAMS
HOLD THE FUTURE IN THEIR HANDS.

SUNDAY	MONDAY	TUESDAY
29	30	31
05	06	07
	LABOR/LABOUR DAY (US/CAN)	
12	13	14
19	20	21
26	27	28

WEDNESDAY	THURSDAY	FRIDAY	SATURDAY
01	02	03	04
08	09	10	11
		PATRIOT DAY (US)	
15	16	17	18
22	23	24	25
FIRST DAY OF AUTUMN			
29	30	01	02

August 30 - September 5, 2021

SUBJECT	MONDAY	30	TUESDAY	31	WEDNESDAY	01

Words of Wisdom:

THURSDAY	02	FRIDAY	03	SATURDAY	04

SUNDAY	05

GOALS

- ◯
- ◯
- ◯
- ◯
- ◯
- ◯
- ◯
- ◯

NOTES

September 6 - September 12, 2021

SUBJECT	MONDAY	06	TUESDAY	07	WEDNESDAY	08

THURSDAY	09	FRIDAY	10	SATURDAY	11

SUNDAY | **12**

GOALS

- ○
- ○
- ○
- ○
- ○
- ○
- ○
- ○

NOTES

September 13 – September 19, 2021

SUBJECT	MONDAY	13	TUESDAY	14	WEDNESDAY	15

THURSDAY	16	FRIDAY	17	SATURDAY	18

SUNDAY	19

GOALS

- ○
- ○
- ○
- ○
- ○
- ○
- ○
- ○

NOTES

September 20 - September 26, 2021

SUBJECT	MONDAY	20	TUESDAY	21	WEDNESDAY	22

THURSDAY	23	FRIDAY	24	SATURDAY	25

SUNDAY	26

GOALS

- ○
- ○
- ○
- ○
- ○
- ○
- ○
- ○

NOTES

GOOD THINGS COME TO PEOPLE WHO WAIT, BUT BETTER THINGS COME TO THOSE WHO GO OUT AND GET THEM.

Notes

_____

_____

_____

_____

_____

_____

_____

_____

_____

_____

_____

_____

_____

_____

_____

_____

_____

_____

_____

_____

_____

SUNDAY	MONDAY	TUESDAY
26	27	28
03	04	05
10	11 COLUMBUS DAY (US) THANKSGIVING (CAN)	12
17	18	19
24	25	26
31 HALLOWEEN		

October 2021

WEDNESDAY	THURSDAY	FRIDAY	SATURDAY
29	30	01	02
06	07	08	09
13	14	15	16
20	21	22	23
27	28	29	30

September 27 - October 3, 2021

SUBJECT	MONDAY	27	TUESDAY	28	WEDNESDAY	29

Words of Wisdom: IT TAKES A BIG HEART TO HELP SHAPE LITTLE MINDS.

THURSDAY	30	FRIDAY	01	SATURDAY	02

SUNDAY 03

GOALS

- ○
- ○
- ○
- ○
- ○
- ○
- ○
- ○

NOTES

October 4 - October 10, 2021

SUBJECT	MONDAY	04	TUESDAY	05	WEDNESDAY	06

Words of Wisdom: THE BEST TEACHERS TEACH FROM THE HEART, NOT FROM THE BOOK.

THURSDAY	07	FRIDAY	08	SATURDAY	09

SUNDAY	10

GOALS

- ◯
- ◯
- ◯
- ◯
- ◯
- ◯
- ◯
- ◯

NOTES

October 11 - October 17, 2021

SUBJECT	MONDAY	11	TUESDAY	12	WEDNESDAY	13

THURSDAY	14	FRIDAY	15	SATURDAY	16

SUNDAY	17

GOALS

- ○
- ○
- ○
- ○
- ○
- ○
- ○
- ○

NOTES

October 18 - October 24, 2021

SUBJECT	MONDAY	18	TUESDAY	19	WEDNESDAY	20

Words of Wisdom:

THURSDAY	21	FRIDAY	22	SATURDAY	23

SUNDAY	24

GOALS

- ◯
- ◯
- ◯
- ◯
- ◯
- ◯
- ◯
- ◯

NOTES

October 25 - October 31, 2021

SUBJECT	MONDAY	25	TUESDAY	26	WEDNESDAY	27

Words of Wisdom: THE BEST TEACHERS ARE THOSE WHO TELL YOU WHERE TO LOOK, BUT DON'T TELL YOU WHAT TO SEE.

THURSDAY	28	FRIDAY	29	SATURDAY	30

SUNDAY	31

GOALS

- ○
- ○
- ○
- ○
- ○
- ○
- ○
- ○

NOTES

Notes

_____

_____

_____

_____

_____

_____

_____

_____

_____

_____

_____

_____

_____

_____

_____

_____

_____

_____

_____

_____

_____

_____

_____

SUNDAY	MONDAY	TUESDAY
31	01	02
07	08	09
DAYLIGHT SAVING TIME ENDS		
14	15	16
21	22	23
28	29	30

November 2021

WEDNESDAY	THURSDAY	FRIDAY	SATURDAY
03	04	05	06
10	11	12	13
	VETERAN'S DAY (US) REMEMBRANCE DAY (CAN)		
17	18	19	20
24	25	26	27
	THANKSGIVING (US)		
01	02	03	04

November 1 - November 7, 2021

SUBJECT	MONDAY	01	TUESDAY	02	WEDNESDAY	03

Words of Wisdom: TEACHERS WHO LOVE TEACHING TEACH CHILDREN TO LOVE LEARNING.

THURSDAY	04	FRIDAY	05	SATURDAY	06

SUNDAY 07

GOALS

- ◯
- ◯
- ◯
- ◯
- ◯
- ◯
- ◯
- ◯

NOTES

November 8 - November 14, 2021

SUBJECT	MONDAY	08	TUESDAY	09	WEDNESDAY	10

Words of Wisdom:

A TRULY GREAT TEACHER IS HARD TO FIND,
DIFFICULT TO PART WITH AND IMPOSSIBLE TO FORGET.

THURSDAY	11	FRIDAY	12	SATURDAY	13

SUNDAY	14

GOALS

- ◯
- ◯
- ◯
- ◯
- ◯
- ◯
- ◯
- ◯

NOTES

November 15 - November 21, 2021

SUBJECT	MONDAY	15	TUESDAY	16	WEDNESDAY	17

THURSDAY	18	FRIDAY	19	SATURDAY	20

SUNDAY	21

GOALS

- ◯
- ◯
- ◯
- ◯
- ◯
- ◯
- ◯
- ◯

NOTES

November 22 - November 28, 2021

SUBJECT	MONDAY	22	TUESDAY	23	WEDNESDAY	24

THURSDAY	25	FRIDAY	26	SATURDAY	27

SUNDAY	28

GOALS

- ◯
- ◯
- ◯
- ◯
- ◯
- ◯
- ◯
- ◯

NOTES

THE DEEPEST CRAVING OF HUMAN NATURE IS THE NEED TO BE APPRECIATED.

Notes

SUNDAY	MONDAY	TUESDAY
28	29	30
05	06	07
12	13	14
19	20	21 FIRST DAY OF WINTER
26	27	28

BOXING DAY (CAN/UK)

December 2021

WEDNESDAY	THURSDAY	FRIDAY	SATURDAY
01	02	03	04
08	09	10	11
15	16	17	18
22	23	24 CHRISTMAS EVE	25 CHRISTMAS
29	30	31 NEW YEAR'S EVE	01

November 29 – December 5, 2021

SUBJECT	MONDAY	29	TUESDAY	30	WEDNESDAY	01

Words of Wisdom: THE INFLUENCE OF A GOOD TEACHER CAN NEVER BE ERASED.

THURSDAY	02	FRIDAY	03	SATURDAY	04

SUNDAY 05

GOALS

- ○
- ○
- ○
- ○
- ○
- ○
- ○
- ○

NOTES

December 6 - December 12, 2021

SUBJECT	MONDAY	06	TUESDAY	07	WEDNESDAY	08

THURSDAY	09	FRIDAY	10	SATURDAY	11

SUNDAY | 12

GOALS

- ◯
- ◯
- ◯
- ◯
- ◯
- ◯
- ◯
- ◯

NOTES

December 13 - December 19, 2021

SUBJECT	MONDAY	13	TUESDAY	14	WEDNESDAY	15

THURSDAY	16	FRIDAY	17	SATURDAY	18

SUNDAY 19

GOALS

- ◯
- ◯
- ◯
- ◯
- ◯
- ◯
- ◯
- ◯

NOTES

December 20 – December 26, 2021

SUBJECT	MONDAY	20	TUESDAY	21	WEDNESDAY	22

Words of Wisdom:

THE KIDS WHO NEED THE MOST LOVE WILL OFTEN ASK FOR IT
IN THE MOST UNLOVING WAYS.

THURSDAY	23	FRIDAY	24	SATURDAY	25

SUNDAY 26

GOALS

- ○
- ○
- ○
- ○
- ○
- ○
- ○
- ○

NOTES

Notes

SUNDAY	MONDAY	TUESDAY
26	27	28
02	03	04
09	10	11
16	17 MARTIN LUTHER KING JR. DAY (US)	18
23	24	25
30	31	

WEDNESDAY	THURSDAY	FRIDAY	SATURDAY
29	30	31	01 NEW YEAR'S DAY
05	06	07	08
12	13	14	15
19	20	21	22
26	27	28	29

December 27, 2021 - January 2, 2022

SUBJECT	MONDAY	27	TUESDAY	28	WEDNESDAY	29

THURSDAY	30	FRIDAY	31	SATURDAY	01

SUNDAY	02

GOALS

- ◯
- ◯
- ◯
- ◯
- ◯
- ◯
- ◯
- ◯

NOTES

January 3 - January 9, 2022

SUBJECT	MONDAY	03	TUESDAY	04	WEDNESDAY	05

THURSDAY	06	FRIDAY	07	SATURDAY	08

SUNDAY — 09

GOALS

- ○
- ○
- ○
- ○
- ○
- ○
- ○
- ○

NOTES

January 10 - January 16, 2022

SUBJECT	MONDAY	10	TUESDAY	11	WEDNESDAY	12

I HAVE THE ABILITY TO CHANGE MY STUDENT'S LIVES,
I WON'T WASTE IT.

THURSDAY	13	FRIDAY	14	SATURDAY	15

SUNDAY 16

GOALS

○
○
○
○
○
○
○
○

NOTES

January 17 - January 23, 2022

SUBJECT	MONDAY	17	TUESDAY	18	WEDNESDAY	19

Words of Wisdom:

TEACHERS ARE THE ONLY ONES WHO LOSE SLEEP OVER OTHER PEOPLE'S CHILDREN.

THURSDAY	20	FRIDAY	21	SATURDAY	22

SUNDAY 23

GOALS

- ⚪
- ⚪
- ⚪
- ⚪
- ⚪
- ⚪
- ⚪
- ⚪

NOTES

January 24 - January 30, 2022

SUBJECT	MONDAY	24	TUESDAY	25	WEDNESDAY	26

THURSDAY	27	FRIDAY	28	SATURDAY	29

SUNDAY 30

GOALS

- ◯
- ◯
- ◯
- ◯
- ◯
- ◯
- ◯
- ◯

NOTES

Notes

_____

_____

_____

_____

_____

_____

_____

_____

_____

_____

_____

_____

_____

_____

_____

_____

SUNDAY	MONDAY	TUESDAY
30	31	01
06	07	08
13	14	15
	VALENTINE'S DAY	
20	21	22
	PRESIDENT'S DAY (US)	
27	28	01

february 2022

WEDNESDAY	THURSDAY	FRIDAY	SATURDAY
02	03	04	05
09	10	11	12
16	17	18	19
23	24	25	26
02	03	04	05

January 31 - February 6, 2022

SUBJECT	MONDAY	31	TUESDAY	01	WEDNESDAY	02

THURSDAY	03	FRIDAY	04	SATURDAY	05

SUNDAY	06

GOALS

- ○
- ○
- ○
- ○
- ○
- ○
- ○
- ○

NOTES

february 7 - february 13, 2022

SUBJECT	MONDAY	07	TUESDAY	08	WEDNESDAY	09

Words of Wisdom:

THURSDAY	10	FRIDAY	11	SATURDAY	12

SUNDAY	13

GOALS

- ○
- ○
- ○
- ○
- ○
- ○
- ○
- ○

NOTES

february 14 - february 20, 2022

SUBJECT	MONDAY	14	TUESDAY	15	WEDNESDAY	16

Words of Wisdom: EVERY STUDENT IS CAPABLE OF LEARNING, JUST NOT ON THE SAME DAY OR IN THE SAME WAY.

THURSDAY	17	FRIDAY	18	SATURDAY	19

SUNDAY	20

GOALS

- ○
- ○
- ○
- ○
- ○
- ○
- ○
- ○

NOTES

february 21 - february 27, 2022

SUBJECT	MONDAY	21	TUESDAY	22	WEDNESDAY	23

Words of Wisdom:

THURSDAY	24	FRIDAY	25	SATURDAY	26

SUNDAY 27

GOALS

- ◯
- ◯
- ◯
- ◯
- ◯
- ◯
- ◯
- ◯

NOTES

Notes

_____

_____

_____

_____

_____

_____

_____

_____

_____

_____

_____

_____

_____

_____

_____

_____

_____

_____

_____

_____

SUNDAY	MONDAY	TUESDAY
27	28	01
06	07	08
13	14	15
DAYLIGHT SAVING TIME BEGINS		
20	21	22
FIRST DAY OF SPRING		
27	28	29

WEDNESDAY	THURSDAY	FRIDAY	SATURDAY
02	03	04	05
09	10	11	12
16	17	18	19
	ST. PATRICK'S DAY		
23	24	25	26
30	31	01	02

february 28 - March 6, 2022

SUBJECT	MONDAY	28	TUESDAY	01	WEDNESDAY	02

Words of Wisdom: WHEN ONE TEACHES, TWO LEARN. -ROBERT HEINLEIN

THURSDAY	03	FRIDAY	04	SATURDAY	05

SUNDAY | 06

GOALS

- ◯
- ◯
- ◯
- ◯
- ◯
- ◯
- ◯
- ◯

NOTES

March 7 - March 13, 2022

SUBJECT	MONDAY	07	TUESDAY	08	WEDNESDAY	09

THURSDAY	10	FRIDAY	11	SATURDAY	12

SUNDAY	13

GOALS

- ◯
- ◯
- ◯
- ◯
- ◯
- ◯
- ◯
- ◯

NOTES

March 14 - March 20, 2022

SUBJECT	MONDAY	14	TUESDAY	15	WEDNESDAY	16

Words of Wisdom: WHAT YOU TEACH TODAY MAY SOMEDAY LIGHT THE WORLD.
-L.W. FOX

THURSDAY	17	FRIDAY	18	SATURDAY	19

SUNDAY	20

GOALS

- ○
- ○
- ○
- ○
- ○
- ○
- ○
- ○

NOTES

March 21 - March 27, 2022

SUBJECT	MONDAY	21	TUESDAY	22	WEDNESDAY	23

THURSDAY	24	FRIDAY	25	SATURDAY	26

SUNDAY 27

GOALS

- ○
- ○
- ○
- ○
- ○
- ○
- ○
- ○

NOTES

THE WONDERFUL THING ABOUT LEARNING IS
NO ONE CAN TAKE IT AWAY FROM YOU.

Notes

_____

_____

_____

_____

_____

_____

_____

_____

_____

_____

_____

_____

_____

_____

_____

_____

_____

_____

SUNDAY	MONDAY	TUESDAY
27	28	29
03	04	05
10	11	12
17	18	19
EASTER	EASTER MONDAY	
24	25	26

April 2022

WEDNESDAY	THURSDAY	FRIDAY	SATURDAY
30	31	01	02
06	07	08	09
13	14	15	16
		GOOD FRIDAY	
20	21	22	23
27	28	29	30

March 28 - April 3, 2022

SUBJECT	MONDAY	28	TUESDAY	29	WEDNESDAY	30

Words of Wisdom: IF YOU WANT TO BE AN OPTIMIST, BECOME A TEACHER.

THURSDAY	31	FRIDAY	01	SATURDAY	02

SUNDAY | 03

GOALS

- ◯
- ◯
- ◯
- ◯
- ◯
- ◯
- ◯
- ◯

NOTES

April 4 - April 10, 2022

SUBJECT	MONDAY	04	TUESDAY	05	WEDNESDAY	06

THURSDAY	07	FRIDAY	08	SATURDAY	09

SUNDAY | 10

GOALS

- ◯
- ◯
- ◯
- ◯
- ◯
- ◯
- ◯
- ◯

NOTES

April 11 – April 17, 2022

SUBJECT	MONDAY	11	TUESDAY	12	WEDNESDAY	13

Words of Wisdom: EDUCATION BREEDS CONFIDENCE. CONFIDENCE BREEDS HOPE. HOPE BREEDS PEACE. -CONFUCIUS

THURSDAY	14	FRIDAY	15	SATURDAY	16

SUNDAY	17

GOALS

- ◯
- ◯
- ◯
- ◯
- ◯
- ◯
- ◯
- ◯

NOTES

April 18 – April 24, 2022

SUBJECT	MONDAY	18	TUESDAY	19	WEDNESDAY	20

Words of Wisdom: THE FUTURE OF THE WORLD IS IN MY CLASSROOM TODAY.

THURSDAY	21	FRIDAY	22	SATURDAY	23

SUNDAY · 24

GOALS

- ◯
- ◯
- ◯
- ◯
- ◯
- ◯
- ◯
- ◯

NOTES

April 25 - May 1, 2022

SUBJECT	MONDAY	25	TUESDAY	26	WEDNESDAY	27

THURSDAY	28	FRIDAY	29	SATURDAY	30

SUNDAY	01

GOALS

- ○
- ○
- ○
- ○
- ○
- ○
- ○
- ○

NOTES

WISDOM COMES NOT FROM AGE,
BUT FROM EDUCATION AND LEARNING. -ANTON CHEKHOV

Notes

SUNDAY	MONDAY	TUESDAY
01	02	03
	MAY DAY (UK)	
08	09	10
MOTHER'S DAY		
15	16	17
22	23	24
	VICTORIA DAY (CAN)	
29	30	31
	MEMORIAL DAY (US)	

May 2022

WEDNESDAY	THURSDAY	FRIDAY	SATURDAY
04	05	06	07
	CINCO DE MAYO		
11	12	13	14
18	19	20	21
25	26	27	28
01	02	03	04

May 2 - May 8, 2022

SUBJECT	MONDAY	02	TUESDAY	03	WEDNESDAY	04

Words of Wisdom: EVERY DAY MAY NOT BE GOOD BUT THERE IS GOOD IN EVERY DAY.

THURSDAY	05	FRIDAY	06	SATURDAY	07

SUNDAY	08

GOALS

- ○
- ○
- ○
- ○
- ○
- ○
- ○
- ○

NOTES

May 9 - May 15, 2022

SUBJECT	MONDAY	09	TUESDAY	10	WEDNESDAY	11

THURSDAY	12	FRIDAY	13	SATURDAY	14

SUNDAY	15

GOALS

- ◯
- ◯
- ◯
- ◯
- ◯
- ◯
- ◯
- ◯

NOTES

May 16 - May 22, 2022

SUBJECT	MONDAY	16	TUESDAY	17	WEDNESDAY	18

THURSDAY	19	FRIDAY	20	SATURDAY	21

SUNDAY 22

GOALS

- ◯
- ◯
- ◯
- ◯
- ◯
- ◯
- ◯
- ◯

NOTES

May 23 - May 29, 2022

SUBJECT	MONDAY	23	TUESDAY	24	WEDNESDAY	25

Words of Wisdom: TODAY IS A GOOD DAY TO HAVE A GREAT DAY.

THURSDAY	26	FRIDAY	27	SATURDAY	28

SUNDAY 29

GOALS

- ○
- ○
- ○
- ○
- ○
- ○
- ○
- ○

NOTES

FIND HARMONY IN WHAT YOU THINK, SAY AND DO, THEN YOU WILL FIND HAPPINESS.

Notes

_____

_____

_____

_____

_____

_____

_____

_____

_____

_____

_____

_____

_____

_____

_____

_____

_____

_____

_____

_____

_____

_____

_____

SUNDAY	MONDAY	TUESDAY
29	30	31
05	06	07
12	13	14
19 FATHER'S DAY JUNETEENTH (US)	20	21 FIRST DAY OF SUMMER
26	27	28

WEDNESDAY	THURSDAY	FRIDAY	SATURDAY
01	02	03	04
	SPRING BANK HOLIDAY (UK)		
08	09	10	11
15	16	17	18
22	23	24	25
29	30	01	02

May 30 - June 5, 2022

SUBJECT	MONDAY	30	TUESDAY	31	WEDNESDAY	01

Words of Wisdom:

THURSDAY	02	FRIDAY	03	SATURDAY	04

SUNDAY	05

GOALS

- ◯
- ◯
- ◯
- ◯
- ◯
- ◯
- ◯
- ◯

NOTES

June 6 - June 12, 2022

SUBJECT	MONDAY	06	TUESDAY	07	WEDNESDAY	08

THURSDAY	09	FRIDAY	10	SATURDAY	11

SUNDAY 12

GOALS

- ◯
- ◯
- ◯
- ◯
- ◯
- ◯
- ◯
- ◯

NOTES

June 13 - June 19, 2022

SUBJECT	MONDAY	13	TUESDAY	14	WEDNESDAY	15

Words of Wisdom:

THURSDAY	16	FRIDAY	17	SATURDAY	18

SUNDAY	19

GOALS

- ◯
- ◯
- ◯
- ◯
- ◯
- ◯
- ◯
- ◯

NOTES

June 20 – June 26, 2022

SUBJECT	MONDAY	20	TUESDAY	21	WEDNESDAY	22

Words of Wisdom:
I AM A PERSON OF HIGH INTEGRITY AND SINCERE PURPOSE.

THURSDAY	23	FRIDAY	24	SATURDAY	25

SUNDAY	26

GOALS

- ○
- ○
- ○
- ○
- ○
- ○
- ○
- ○

NOTES

Notes

SUNDAY	MONDAY	TUESDAY
26	27	28
03	04	05
	INDEPENDENCE DAY (US)	
10	11	12
17	18	19
24	25	26
31		

July 2022

WEDNESDAY	THURSDAY	FRIDAY	SATURDAY
29	30	01	02
		CANADA DAY (CAN)	
06	07	08	09
13	14	15	16
20	21	22	23
27	28	29	30

June 27 - July 3, 2022

SUBJECT	MONDAY	27	TUESDAY	28	WEDNESDAY	29

Words of Wisdom:

EVERY CHILD IS ONE CARING ADULT AWAY
FROM BEING A SUCCESS STORY.

THURSDAY	30	FRIDAY	01	SATURDAY	02

SUNDAY	03

GOALS

- ◯
- ◯
- ◯
- ◯
- ◯
- ◯
- ◯
- ◯

NOTES

July 4 - July 10, 2022

SUBJECT	MONDAY	04	TUESDAY	05	WEDNESDAY	06

EDUCATION IS WHAT REMAINS WHEN YOU'VE FORGOTTEN
EVERYTHING YOU'VE LEARNED.

THURSDAY	07	FRIDAY	08	SATURDAY	09

SUNDAY | 10

GOALS

- ◯
- ◯
- ◯
- ◯
- ◯
- ◯
- ◯
- ◯

NOTES

July 11 – July 17, 2022

SUBJECT	MONDAY	11	TUESDAY	12	WEDNESDAY	13

Words of Wisdom:

THURSDAY	14	FRIDAY	15	SATURDAY	16

SUNDAY 17

GOALS

- ○
- ○
- ○
- ○
- ○
- ○
- ○
- ○

NOTES

July 18 - July 24, 2022

SUBJECT	MONDAY	18	TUESDAY	19	WEDNESDAY	20

SUBJECT	MONDAY	18	TUESDAY	19	WEDNESDAY	20

THURSDAY	21	FRIDAY	22	SATURDAY	23

SUNDAY | 24

GOALS

- ◯
- ◯
- ◯
- ◯
- ◯
- ◯
- ◯
- ◯

NOTES

July 25 - July 31, 2022

SUBJECT	MONDAY	25	TUESDAY	26	WEDNESDAY	27

Words of Wisdom:

THURSDAY	28	FRIDAY	29	SATURDAY	30

SUNDAY	31

GOALS

- ○
- ○
- ○
- ○
- ○
- ○
- ○
- ○

NOTES

Notes

Notes

Notes

Notes

Notes

Notes